Indiana

BY AMY VAN ZEE

The
Child's
World®

Published by The Child's World®
1980 Lookout Drive • Mankato, MN 56003-1705
800-599-READ • www.childsworld.com

ACKNOWLEDGMENTS
The Child's World®: Mary Berendes, Publishing Director
The Design Lab: Design and production
Red Line Editorial: Editorial direction

PHOTO CREDITS: Jan Paul Schrage/iStockphoto, cover, 1, 3; Matt Kania/Map
Hero, Inc., 4, 5; Ken Cave/Shutterstock Images, 7; Kenneth Keifer/Shutterstock
Images, 9; iStockphoto, 10, 13; Oscar Gutierrez/iStockphoto, 11; North Wind
Picture Archives/Photolibrary, 15; Diego Alvarez de Toledo/iStockphoto, 17;
Charles Dharapak/AP Images, 19; Jeff Roberson/AP Images, 21; One Mile Up,
22; Quarter-dollar coin image from the United States Mint, 22

LIBRARY OF CONGRESS CATALOGING-IN-PUBLICATION DATA
Van Zee, Amy.
  Indiana / by Amy Van Zee.
     p. cm.
  Includes bibliographical references and index.
  ISBN 978-1-60253-458-2 (library bound : alk. paper)
  1. Indiana—Juvenile literature. I. Title.

F526.3.V36 2010
977.2—dc22

2010017676

Printed in the United States of America in Mankato, Minnesota.
July 2010
F11538

On the cover: People
in Indiana enjoy
race car driving.

CONTENTS

Geography

Let's explore Indiana! Indiana is in the central United States. This area is called the Midwest. Lake Michigan lies to the north of Indiana. It is one of the five Great Lakes.

Lake Michigan

MICHIGAN

Michigan City

South Bend

Gary Portage

Nappanee

Fort Wayne

ILLINOIS

Monticello

Battle Ground

Kokomo

Lafayette

INDIANA

Muncie

Fishers

OHIO

⭐ **Indianapolis**

Cataract Falls

Brown County State Park

Brookville

Bloomington

Ohio River

Wabash River

Vincennes

New Albany

Evansville

NORTH EAST SOUTH WEST

KENTUCKY

Cities

Indianapolis is the capital of Indiana. It is also the largest city in the state. Fort Wayne and Evansville are other large cities.

Indianapolis is home to about 800,000 people. ▶

Land

The Wabash River and the Ohio River make up two of Indiana's borders. Much of Indiana's land has rich soil. This makes it good for farming. In the north, the land is mostly rolling hills. In the south, the land has many hills and valleys.

Lower Cataract Falls is part of the larger Cataract Falls, the largest waterfall in Indiana. ▶

Plants and Animals

Indiana's state tree is the tulip tree, which grows very tall. It is also known as the yellow poplar. The state flower is the peony. Peonies can be white, red, pink, or a mix of these colors. The state bird of Indiana is the cardinal. Male cardinals are often red with black markings near the eyes. These markings look like a mask. Females are often brown and red.

Peonies **bloom** from late May to early June. ▶

People and Work

More than 6 million people live in Indiana. Many people work in **manufacturing**. They make **products** from iron and steel. These products include cars and car parts. Farming is also important in Indiana. Crops include corn and wheat.

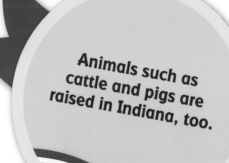

Animals such as cattle and pigs are raised in Indiana, too.

This factory in Indianapolis makes **chemicals**. ▶

13

History

French explorers came to this area in the 1600s. At the time, many Native American **tribes** lived here. Indiana became a U.S. **territory** in 1800. Indiana became the nineteenth state on December 11, 1816.

The Shawnee is one Native American tribe that has lived in Indiana. ▶

Ways of Life

Many people in Indiana enjoy playing and watching sports such as basketball, football, and race car driving. Some people enjoy outdoor activities, such as **hiking** and camping. Indiana has national parks to visit, too. Visitors can learn about Indiana's history and explore nature.

Family members enjoy camping together in Indiana. ▶

Famous People

Actor James Dean was born in Indiana. So was basketball player Larry Bird. Television host David Letterman was born in Indiana, too.

David Letterman is the host of the ▶
Late Show with David Letterman.

19

Famous Places

Indiana is home to the Indianapolis Motor **Speedway**. This racetrack hosts the Indianapolis 500, a famous car race. Indiana is also home to well-known colleges and universities. The University of Notre Dame and Purdue University are in Indiana.

Thousands of fans watch the Indianapolis 500, which is held each spring. ▶

State Symbols

Seal

Indiana's state seal shows a man chopping down a tree. Many believe this stands for settlers clearing land in the West. Go to childsworld.com/links for a link to Indiana's state Web site, where you can get a firsthand look at the state seal.

Flag

The 19 stars on the state flag stand for Indiana being the nineteenth state.

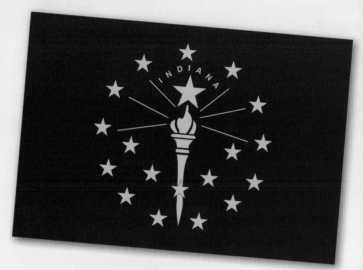

Quarter

A race car on the Indiana state quarter stands for the Indianapolis 500. The quarter came out in 2002.

Glossary

bloom (BLOOM): If things bloom, they open up. Peonies, Indiana's state flower, bloom in summer.

chemicals (KEM-uh-kulz): Chemicals are substances used in chemistry. Some factories in Indiana make chemicals.

hiking (HYK-ing): Hiking is taking a walk in a natural area, such as a hill or a mountain. People enjoy hiking in Indiana.

manufacturing (man-yuh-FAK-chur-ing): Manufacturing is the task of making items with machines. Many people in Indiana work in manufacturing.

products (PROD-ukts): Products are things that are made by people. Some people who work in manufacturing make products out of steel and iron.

seal (SEEL): A seal is a symbol a state uses for government business. A man chopping down a tree is shown on the Indiana state seal.

speedway (SPEED-way): A speedway is a racetrack for cars. The Indianapolis Motor Speedway is in Indiana.

symbols (SIM-bulz): Symbols are pictures or things that stand for something else. The seal and flag are Indiana's symbols.

territory (TAYR-uh-tor-ee): A territory is a piece of land that is controlled by another country. Indiana became a U.S. territory in 1800.

tribes (TRYBZ): Tribes are groups of people who share ancestors and customs. Many Native American tribes lived in the Indiana area when the first European explorers came.

Further Information

Books

Dennis, Yvonne Wakim, and Arlene Hirschfelder. *A Kids' Guide to Native American History*. Chicago: Chicago Review Press, 2010.

Hyde, Judith Jensen. *Indiana*. New York: Children's Press, 2007.

Reynolds, Cynthia Furlong. *H is for Hoosier: An Indiana Alphabet*. Chelsea, MI: Sleeping Bear Press, 2001.

Web Sites

Visit our Web site for links about Indiana: *childsworld.com/links*

Note to Parents, Teachers, and Librarians: We routinely verify our Web links to make sure they are safe and active sites. So encourage your readers to check them out!

Index